OSTRICHES

by

HERBERT S. ZIM

illustrated by

RUSSELL FRANCIS PETERSON

WILLIAM MORROW AND CO.
NEW YORK   1958

Birds live from the cold Arctic to the even colder Antarctic—and nearly everywhere in between. Over 30,000 different kinds of birds are known and all but one tenth of one per cent of them can fly.

Of all things which make birds different from other animals, their feathers and their wings for flying are the most important. So it is indeed strange that there are any birds at all that cannot fly.

Of all the backboned animals, only three groups have learned to fly. These are the extinct flying reptiles known as pterodactyls, the bats, and the birds. The very first bird was a great improvement over the flying reptiles. One of these first birds died and was buried

Pterodactyl wing is its arm and overgrown little finger.

Bird wing is its arm and a hand reduced to three short fingers.

Bat wing is its arm and five long fingers.

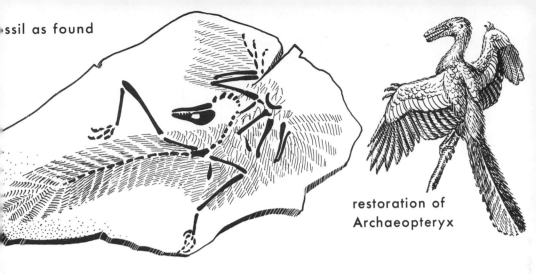

restoration of
Archaeopteryx

in the soft mud of a Bavarian swamp about a hundred million years ago. The fossil imprints of its feathers and bones show that it had well-formed wings and feathers and could certainly fly. Birds have flown ever since.

The few birds which do not fly today are descendants of those which did fly in the distant past. There are two groups of flightless birds now alive—the penguin group and the ostrich group. These birds lost the power of flight a long time ago, before birds had developed into the many different and varied kinds we know.

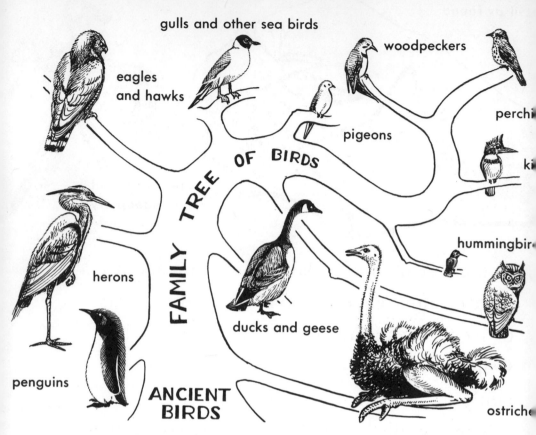

gulls and other sea birds

eagles
and hawks

woodpeckers

perchi

pigeons

ki

FAMILY TREE OF BIRDS

herons

hummingbir

ducks and geese

penguins

ANCIENT
BIRDS

ostriche

Ostriches and their kin are classified by experts as the most simple group of living birds. The only group that is classified lower on the family tree of birds is the group of toothed birds, all of which died off millions of years ago. So ostriches and their relatives form the oldest and simplest group of birds alive today.

This does not mean that ostriches are simple in the same way that a bicycle can be considered a simpler vehicle than an automobile. It means that the development of most birds has, over millions of years, moved in a different way from the development of ostriches.

Most flightless birds are leftovers from past ages. They are interesting but are less well adapted to life today.

The members of the penguin group, the first flightless birds, live mainly in the south temperate and antarctic areas. They are excellent swimmers, with wings that are reduced to flippers. Penguin wings cannot bend like wings of all other birds. They move at the shoulder joint only. In the water, penguins are quick and agile. On land, they move slowly, with a clumsy, amusing gait.

Gentoo penguins

emperor penguins

Adélie penguins

The ostriches and their kin—rheas, cassowaries, emus, and kiwis—form the second and larger group of flightless birds. It is curious that they, too, live mainly in the Southern Hemisphere.

Scientists feel sure that once, long ago, the ancestors of the ostriches could fly. But the way ostriches lived and the way they fed, century after century, put less and less value on the use of wings and more and more value on their legs. So the ostriches that lived, bred, and survived gradually became those which were flightless. Many other kinds of birds have come to depend on their legs more than their wings. Quail and road runners are good examples. However, these birds can fly if they have to. In the ostrich group, the power of flight has been completely lost.

BIRDS THAT SELDOM FLY

bobwhite quail

road runner

Carolina rail
Other rails cannot fly at all.

Ostriches and their kin make up a large group of birds called a superorder. In this group are eight orders of birds—five alive and three extinct. One authority lists a total of nineteen species of flightless birds in these five orders.

The most important difference between the ostrich group and other birds is that ostriches and their relatives have a breastbone without a keel. You have seen this keeled breastbone when you have eaten chicken, duck, or turkey, all of which are flying birds. A high ridge ex-

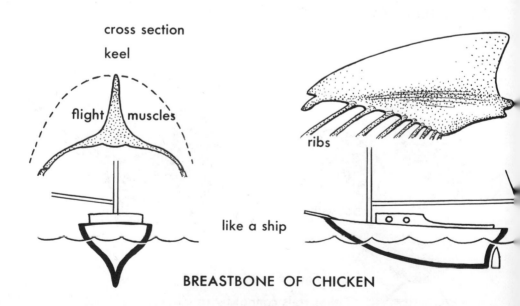

cross section
keel

flight muscles

like a ship

ribs

BREASTBONE OF CHICKEN

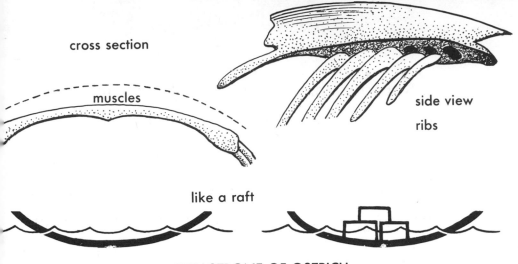

cross section

muscles

side view

ribs

like a raft

BREASTBONE OF OSTRICH

tends the length of the breastbone, and to this ridge are attached the powerful pectoral muscles which birds use in flight. These pectoral muscles are, of course, the white meat which so many people like.

The ostrich group has a flat breastbone that looks more like a raft than like a boat with a keel. This raftlike breastbone gives the scientific name to this entire group of birds. They are classified as *Ratitae,* from the Latin word *ratis,* a raft.

Another characteristic of the ostrich group is that the diaphragm is better developed than in other birds. You have a diaphragm and so do all mammals. This is a thin, tough sheet of tissue right below your ribs. It separates your lungs from your stomach, liver, and other organs of digestion.

Muscles are attached around the edge of the diaphragm and, in breathing, the diaphragm moves up and down. This helps pump air in

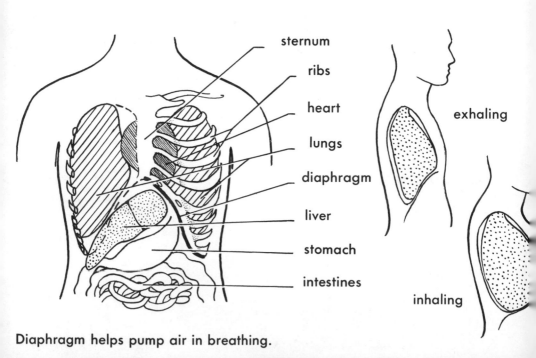

sternum

ribs

heart

lungs

diaphragm

liver

stomach

intestines

exhaling

inhaling

Diaphragm helps pump air in breathing.

and out of your lungs. Neither the lungs nor the diaphragm of most birds are as well developed as those of mammals, but this is not true of the ostrich group.

The shoulder bones, or clavicles, of flying birds come together and join at the front end of the breastbone keel, forming the wishbone. However, if you look for a wishbone the next time you eat ostrich (and it was once prized as a delicacy), you will look in vain, for the wishbone does not exist in the ostrich or other ratite birds.

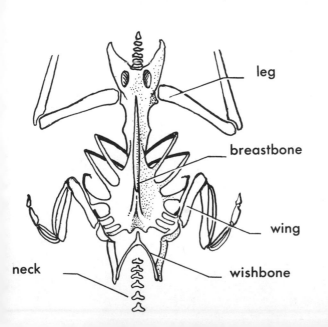

neck
leg
breastbone
wing
wishbone

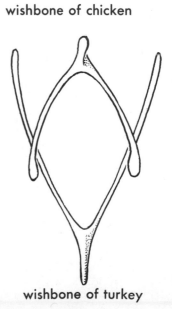

wishbone of chicken

wishbone of turkey

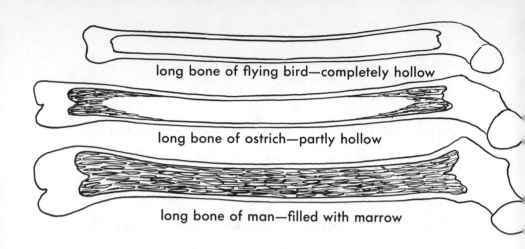

long bone of flying bird—completely hollow

long bone of ostrich—partly hollow

long bone of man—filled with marrow

There is one more matter of bones worth noting. The long bones of flying birds are almost completely hollow. This emptiness makes the bones much lighter, yet even stronger than if they were solid. Your long bones (like those of your arms and legs) are not hollow inside. The inside is made of much softer material than the outside. The inside of your bones is filled with marrow, and it is here that some of your red blood cells are made. The long bones of ostriches are somewhat like those of mammals but also like those of flying birds—they are partly hollow.

Finally, there is the one thing that makes all birds different from other animals—the feathers that grow from their skins. Feathers probably developed from the flattened scales of reptiles. Legs of birds are still covered with such scales, just like the legs of turtles or of lizards. The feathers of birds grow from living cells, but they themselves are not alive. It would hurt a bird if you pulled out a feather, but it would not hurt if you cut it off.

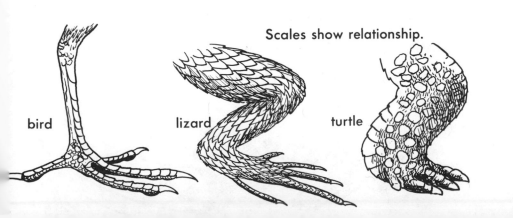

Scales show relationship.

bird   lizard   turtle

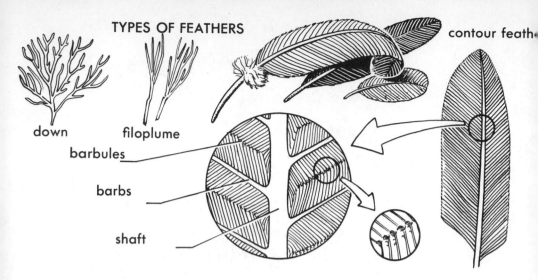

TYPES OF FEATHERS

down

filoplume

barbules

barbs

shaft

contour feather

The feathers which you see when you look at a bird are *contour* feathers. They give the bird its shape. Some of these contour feathers are larger and longer than others, as on the wings and tail. These are the ones used for flying.

Flight feathers are a marvel to see if you look closely. A straight shaft runs down the middle. Extending from both sides of it are the barbs. These in turn have barbules or tiny barbs. The barbules overlap and hook together, forming a tight surface.

The ostrich and its kin have contour feathers, of course, but these do not develop as they do in the flying birds. The barbs do not hook together, and so the feathers remain plumelike. They are very beautiful, but of little value to the ostrich.

The contour feathers do not grow helter-skelter over the skin of most flying birds, but from several distinct tracts, or paths. Skin between these tracts does not produce contour feathers and so is naked. However, the contour feathers of ostriches, and a few other birds, do not follow a clear-cut path, but are spread evenly over the bird's entire body.

crow

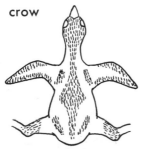

Feathers sprout in this pattern.

ostrich

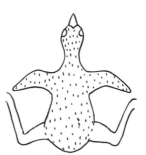

Feathers sprout all over.

These differences, big and small, set the ostrich group apart from other birds. They are important to scientists who are trying to discover how the different kinds of birds came to be, and why they live as they do.

Ostriches live in the dry open plains of Africa. Some are also found in Arabia. Wild or tame, the male ostrich is a handsome bird, black, almost glossy, with white tips to his wings and his tail. His head pivots on a long neck. His flattened bill is strong and heavy. Beady black eyes are always alert. He has heavy thighs and long legs ending in two thick toes.

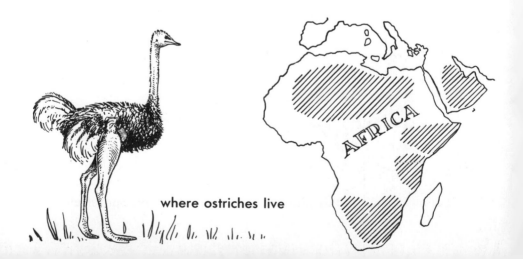

where ostriches live

He is perhaps at his best when courting. Then he stretches himself to his full height and calls with loud *booms*—two short and one long—sometimes keeping this up hour after hour. Often he will follow up his courting by showing off before the drab-looking hen. He will drop to his "knees" and roll back and forth, swaying from left to right with his head down, raising first one wing and then the other. The hen watches but rarely tries to imitate the bowing and rolling of the cock.

The family group of wild ostriches may consist of the cock and three or four hens. After mating, a nest is made, though this is rarely more than a slight hollow in the sand, usually near shrubs and brush. The hen begins to lay, and usually lays one egg every other day. Each egg may be up to eight inches long. Some weigh up to three pounds. Ostrich eggs have quite thick shells speckled with tiny pores. They are glossy and creamy white.

STRICH EGG

side   1   8 9 10 11   front

If a single hen is laying, there may be twelve to fifteen eggs in the nest. If several hens are laying in the same nest, there may be twice or even three times that number. The hens usually set during the day; then the cock takes over and sets during the night. This routine goes on for about six weeks. Then the first eggs begin to hatch. The adult ostriches eat any eggs that are broken in the nest, and sometimes they even eat the first young when they hatch. However, most of the young survive.

By the time an ostrich chick has pecked its way out of the shell, it has worked hard. Most are too weak to stand for a day or so after they hatch, but soon they are up and around, pecking at anything in sight, and eating any grass, seeds, fruits, and insects they can find.

The male bird, who has done his full share in hatching the eggs, keeps an eye on the chicks. So do the hens. They move around together when feeding. The mottled gray and brown of the chicks blend perfectly with the ground. When they squat and are still, they

are impossible to see. Should an enemy approach, the young scatter and hide. The parents may try to lead the intruder away by using the old trick of pretended injury. Otherwise, they stay and fight. An ostrich hisses and rushes at an enemy, pecking hard. When very angry, he kicks dangerously. Ostriches are said to be vicious when on the nest or when caring for their young.

The plump, comical chicks, with thin, wiry feathers, grow rapidly. They are about a foot high when they hatch and grow about a foot a month for six months or so. During their first two years, the male and female birds look alike, but by the third year the adult feathers have appeared. Black and white feathers replace the grayish-brown of the young male bird. The female becomes a soft, gray color. Both have white feathers on the wings and tail. It takes four or five years for an ostrich to reach its full growth. By that time a large male may weigh as much as 300 pounds and may stand eight feet high, but 200 pounds and six feet is a more usual size.

Wild ostrich family groups sometimes mix with herds of antelope and zebra, and feed with them. Ostriches eat all kinds and parts of plants, insects, lizards, small snakes, mice, gophers, and other small mammals. Their appetite is big and they are not fussy about their food. In captivity, ostriches will peck at anything bright or colorful. They have swallowed coins, watches, diamond pins, pencils, and bottle tops.

The wild ostrich is a very timid bird, always on the alert. Its long legs and neck give it a good view of the flat country in which it lives. Hunters or other possible enemies can be spotted at a distance and the alarmed ostrich takes off at high speed.

The very speed of the ostrich has been misunderstood. There is no doubt that the bird is swift. Some people have claimed that ostriches run sixty miles an hour, but more recent estimates place the speed between twenty and thirty miles an hour—which is fast enough.

The ostrich's short wings probably do not help in running. Early observers reported that the ostrich, fleeing from an enemy, raised its wings and used them as a sail or for balance. More recent observers think that the ostrich does nothing of the sort. They say that, when it runs fast, the wind lifts the ostrich's wings because they hang loosely, not because the ostrich is using them in any way.

Another wrong idea is that ostriches are stupid. Their intelligence is no better or worse than that of many other birds. Hunters know that ostriches run in circles when frightened, and use this knowledge to kill or capture them. But people who are lost often wander in circles, too.

ostrich foot

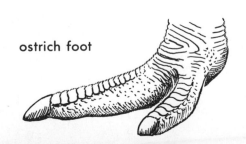

Ostriches do not bury their heads in the sand when they are frightened, as you may have heard. When on the nest they squat low, with heads and necks on the ground. This makes them harder to see. But an old fable dies hard and this one is still being repeated, although no ostrich has even been seen burying its head.

Long before the beginning of history, man learned to tame and domesticate some animals. This great achievement was not accomplished in one step. It was a slow process that took thousands of years. A first step was capturing and taming wild animals. Sometimes the taming was followed by training, so that the animals learned to work with man. Later, some of these animals began to breed in captivity. And only at this stage do they really become domestic animals.

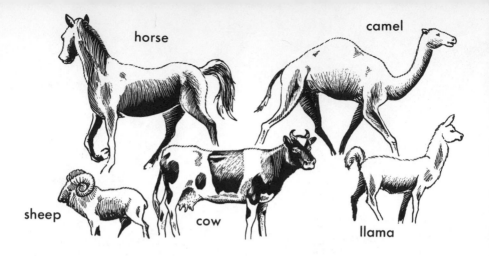

Most of the domestic animals we know were domesticated in ancient times. Dogs may have been domesticated as early as 100,000 years ago. Drawings or carvings of other domesticated animals go back beyond 1000 B.C. The ostrich is one of the few animals which has been domesticated in recent times.

The ancient Egyptians, Arabians, Indians, and Greeks knew about ostriches. Captive birds were sometimes kept in the courts of princes. Arabian hunters captured chicks and raised them in captivity. The birds were kept in small pens and raised for their feathers and meat. But none of this added up to domestication of the ostrich.

ADAPTED FROM LAUFER

It was not until 1865 that the first experiments at domesticating ostriches were made in South Africa. Here, in an area somewhat similar to the American Southwest, the first ostrich farms were established. The birds were given fenced-in grazing land and they thrived, with better food and protection from their few enemies. As the demand for ostrich feathers increased, farmers quickly saw that improving conditions for their ostriches meant better feathers and greater profits.

Gradually, ostriches became truly domesticated birds, and were treated very much like cattle on the farm or on the range. Fertilized eggs were taken from the nests. They were put into incubators just like hens' eggs, and more young were hatched from each batch.

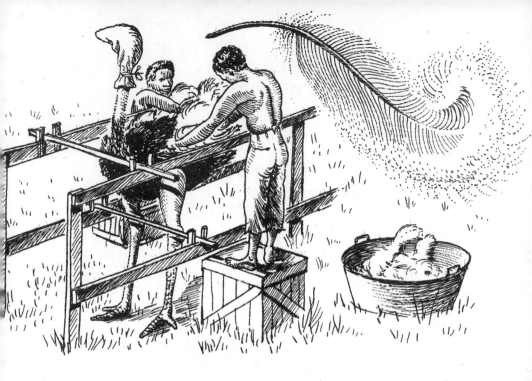

The idea of ostrich farming spread like wildfire. At the height of the ostrich craze, the best grade of feathers brought $250 to $500 a pound. Even less perfect feathers at half the price meant a good profit. A single large ostrich produces a pound of feathers at one clipping and can be clipped every eight or nine months. In 1880, ostriches were taken to Australia, and ostrich farms were started there.

About the same time, 200 prime ostriches were shipped from Capetown, South Africa, to New York by way of Buenos Aires. At New York, the birds were loaded on a train which headed west to Chicago, Omaha, and the Pacific coast. Of the 200 birds starting this voyage of about 23,000 miles, only 22

arrived in southern California, and these were no longer in good health. However, they were the start of the first American ostrich farm.

Later, ostrich farms were started in Arizona, Oklahoma, Texas, Arkansas, and Florida. A few still remain, though changing fashions have made ostrich plumes less important and valuable than they were at the turn of the century.

Of what use is an ostrich? Perhaps it is more useful than a hummingbird and much less than a chicken. Ostrich plumes have been prized since ancient days, when warriors in Africa and Arabia wore them as ornaments. Later, during the crusades, nobles and knights in armor wore plumes proudly. Three ostrich plumes still top the Prince of Wales' emblem.

crest of
Prince of Wales

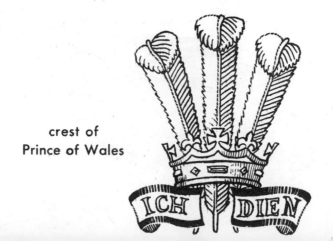

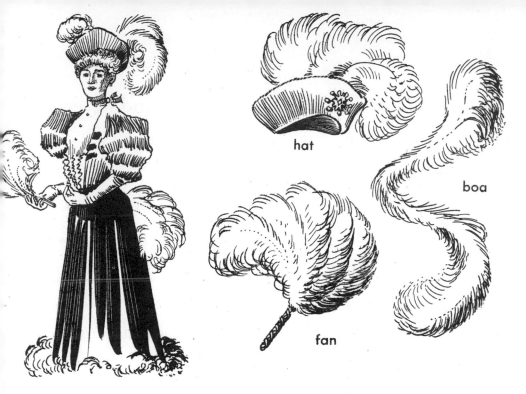

hat

boa

fan

In the last century ostrich plumes became fashionable for ladies' hats, fans, and dress ornaments. That was when ostrich farming began, and fortunes were made (and lost) raising the birds for their feathers. But all that is gone, and ostrich plumes, still beautiful, are more a curiosity now than anything else. Ostrich skin makes a fine, soft leather used for gloves and purses.

Ostrich eggs are good to eat and have often been eaten. Each is equal to about two dozen hens' eggs, but there have never been enough ostrich eggs for people to count on them as a source of food. The idea of eating such a big egg is attractive. One would make an omelette for a large family. But it would take nearly an hour to cook one hard-boiled ostrich egg.

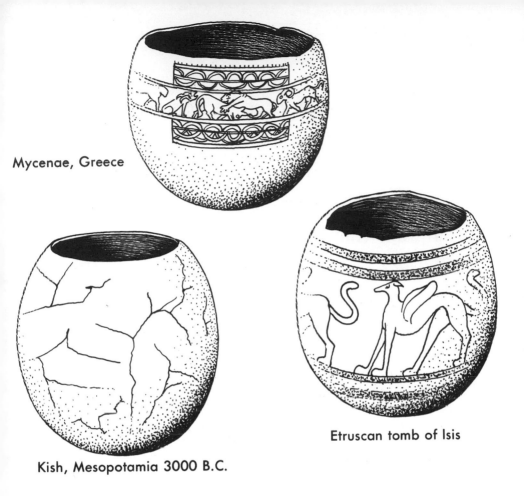

Mycenae, Greece

Kish, Mesopotamia 3000 B.C.

Etruscan tomb of Isis

Another and more interesting use was found for ostrich eggs. Because of their size and beauty, people used to prize them as ornaments. In the days before bottles and glass containers, ostrich eggs were carefully cut open and used as cups. Some were ornamented and engraved with designs around the top and sides. In Assyrian graves, going back to about 3000 B.C., ostrich-egg cups have been found among the owner's possessions which were buried with him. The Egyptians, Chinese, and Greeks also used ostrich eggs for cups and containers.

Not only are ostrich eggs good to eat, but so is the bird itself. It was hunted in Africa by Bushmen who disguised themselves in ostrich feathers. The hunter held up one arm

to imitate the ostrich's head and neck. He moved in such an ostrichlike manner that he could come close enough to the birds to kill one or two of them with his bow and arrow.

Toward the end of the Roman Empire, roast ostrich was a favorite dish at the emperor's table. Roman physicians used ostrich fat as a drug. They thought the stones found in the gizzards were a sure cure for eye diseases.

Large, tame ostriches have been used for racing, with boys or light men as riders. But these birds are not too good in races, since they squat down when they are tired and will run no farther. Ostriches have also been harnessed to light carts and used as beasts of burden. But these odd uses are more for sport than for any real value.

Care is needed to keep ostriches and their relatives from becoming extinct. Most countries where these birds live have passed laws protecting them. They are no longer killed for sport in Africa, Australia, or South America.

Though it is the largest and best known, the ostrich is only one of the group of ratite birds. Others, though less known, were once very common. The rhea is most like the ostrich in appearance. It is a native of South

rheas

America—from Paraguay and southern Brazil, south through the broad pampas to Patagonia. Rheas of several kinds have been identified. All are much smaller than the ostrich—four to five feet high. They also lack the attractive white tail of the African bird. The head and neck of the rhea are completely feathered, unlike the ostrich's. Rheas, like many birds, have three toes, while ostriches have only two.

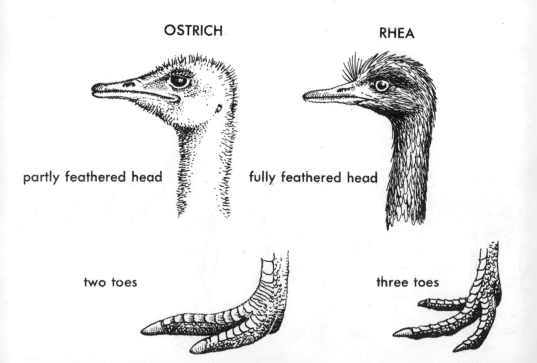

OSTRICH   RHEA

partly feathered head   fully feathered head

two toes   three toes

All the rheas are very similar. Their feathers are grayish-brown, thin and fine, and in one species (Darwin's rhea) are tipped with white. Like the ostrich, rheas seem to get along with other animals. They often travel on the pampas with deer in mixed herds.

Five or six female rheas lay their eggs together in a large nest, but single eggs are laid almost anywhere in the open. By the time the nest has thirty or so eggs, the cock begins to set and he alone takes the responsibility for hatching.

Rheas feed on fruits, berries, and seeds, together with insects and any small animals they can find. Once they were very numerous on the broad, sandy plains of Argentina and Uruguay. The Indians and the Gauchos (the cowboys of this great cattle region) used to hunt them for food or for sport.

bolas

The favorite method of hunting rheas was on horseback with a bola, a weapon consisting of two or three stones, or balls made of lead or wood, tied together at the end of cords six to eight feet long. The bola is whirled around the rider's head somewhat like a lasso and is then thrown. It wraps itself tightly around the legs of the fleeing birds and traps them.

Rhea meat was eaten fresh or dried. The Indians made warm blankets of the skin. Later, in the 1870's, when the ostrich craze was at its height, rheas were killed by the thousands for their feathers. In the middle 1870's, it was estimated that from 300,000 to 500,000 birds were killed each year. Feathers were sent mainly to New York. Some adorned women's hats, but most ended up in feather dusters. The birds rapidly became rare till laws were passed to protect them.

The rhea can stand colder weather than the ostrich. Some have bred in captivity both in England and in Germany. Captive rheas become very tame, and act like overgrown chickens. However, no one has attempted to domesticate rheas as they have ostriches.

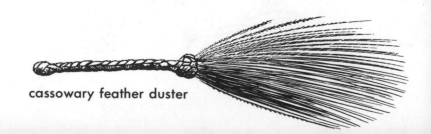

cassowary feather duster

All the ratite birds are wary, but the wariest is the cassowary, which lives in forest and brush lands, feeding at night. These relatives of the ostrich live in Java, Sumatra, and other islands of the East Indies. One kind lives in northeastern Australia.

The several kinds of cassowaries differ quite markedly in their appearance. They are all much smaller than ostriches, usually four to five feet high. Like the rheas they are three-

cassowary foot

toed. All the cassowaries have a bony growth on the skull, and in most of them, this forms a ridge that looks somewhat like an old-fashioned helmet. Cassowaries have no feathers on their heads, which are covered by brilliantly colored skin, usually blue, grading off into brown on the helmet. Most cassowaries also have a colorful wattle or skin growth on the throat.

The cassowary's feathers are thin, and the bird looks as though it might be covered with a coat of long, coarse hair. The wings are very small and are made of only five or six shiny quills. It has no tail at all.

Cassowaries mate during the fall and each female lays a dozen or so greenish eggs in nests of moss or dead leaves. The male sets on the eggs, which hatch in about two months.

Closely related to the cassowaries is the emu, once common to the dry, inland plains of Australia. Now these birds are quite rare. They were hunted as food, for their oil, and for sport until only a few were left.

Emu oil was used to light the lamps of back-country settlers, who also rubbed it on their limbs to relieve aches and pains. It was used in cooking too, and so was emu meat, which travelers said tasted like beef.

emus

The emu itself is more like the cassowary than like any other birds of the ostrich group. It is a bit larger—five to six feet high, but it lacks the ridge or helmet on the top of its head. The bill of the emu is broad and flat. The head of the emu is covered with feathers, and its three-toed feet lack the long, pointed, daggerlike nails of the cassowary. However, the general appearance, the form of the feathers, and the habits of the emu and the cassowary are very much alike.

The color of the emu is a grayish-brown, except for the young birds, which are lighter, with black stripes running from the head down the back. The female lays a dozen or so greenish eggs, about six inches long, in a shallow nest, and, as usual with ratite birds, the male sets on them until they hatch.

kiwi

Strangest of all the ostrichlike birds is the rare kiwi. Only a few are still found in the forests of the two islands which make up New Zealand. Except for its long pointed bill, the kiwi might pass for a miniature emu or rhea. It is only a foot or so high and it lacks both wings and tail. The feathers are thin, coarse, and hairlike. The kiwi has three front toes and, unlike all other ratite birds, a small hind toe. Most birds have their nostrils at the base of the beak. The kiwi's nostrils are at the tip of its six-inch prober.

At dusk or at night, this odd bird walks slowly over the moist forest hillsides, sniffing the ground and poking around the base of plants. It probes into the soft earth for earth-worms—its main food.

This miniature member of the ostrich group lays a very large egg. In proportion to its size,

Kiwi lays the largest egg in proportion to its size.

60 oz.

14½ oz.

the kiwi lays the largest egg of any bird. Sometimes the egg weighs nearly one-quarter the weight of the female.

The last of the ratite birds—the tinamou of southern Brazil and Argentina—is the smallest, barely over a foot tall. It is unlike the others, since it can still fly. When its habits and its structure are studied, however, one can see that the breastbone, skull, and feathers are like those of the ostrich group. It looks something like a partridge.

tinamou

The extinct members of the ostrich group were even more unusual than those now living. Two of the three extinct groups have set their own records in the world of birds. These are the moas and the elephant birds.

The moas, living on both islands of New Zealand, were a large group of birds—probably twenty-five to thirty different kinds. They were all flightless, with small wings or none at all. The smallest moas were the size of tur-

keys. The largest stood eleven or twelve feet high—the largest birds that ever lived.

The moas, which fed mainly or entirely on plants, died off on the North Island of New Zealand perhaps 500 or more years ago. They lived longer on the South Island, and were there when the Maoris came from islands to the north to settle New Zealand. The last ones probably died in the wilder parts of the island 200 to 300 years ago.

Moa bones have been found in swamps and caves. Even bits of skin and feathers have been discovered. From these, scientists have been able to get a good idea of what moas looked like. While some were larger than the ostrich in size, the moas were more closely related to the kiwis. They had four-toed feet like this little bird; not two-toed like the ostrich.

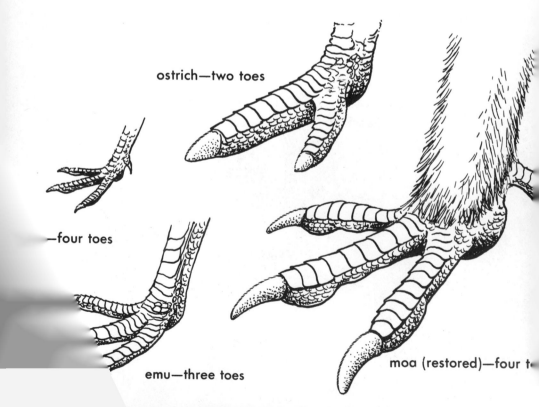

ostrich—two toes

—four toes

emu—three toes

moa (restored)—four t

The elephant birds, called *Aepyronis,* lived in southern Madagascar off the east coast of Africa. There were perhaps as many as thirty different kinds. The largest were probably nine or ten feet high, taller than ostriches and much heavier. Their bones clearly show that these birds had thick, heavy legs.

Elephant birds were probably living when early Arabian explorers reached Madagascar, for these travelers brought back strange tales about a giant bird they called the roc. According to them, this great bird could fly and was so large that it fed on baby elephants. Sinbad, the sailor, was supposed to have been carried off by one.

elephant bird

ostrich

hen

hummingbird

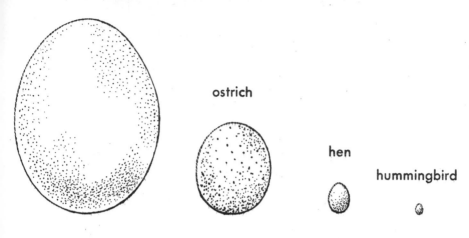

Fossil bones of elephant birds have been found, and fossil eggs also. In the size of its eggs, this bird sets its own record. No bird has ever laid a larger egg. The eggs measured about ten by thirteen inches—with a capacity of more than two gallons. Each equalled 6 to 8 ostrich eggs and 150 to 180 hens' eggs. Natives who found these ancient eggs cut off the tops and used them for water jugs.

Most kinds of ostriches and their kin can be found in the larger zoos. You can see them there and marvel at these creatures which have turned their backs on the rest of the bird world, and have managed to live successfully on the ground for millions upon millions of years.